GREEK

ISLANDS

TRAVEL GUIDE 2025-2026

Discover Timeless Beauty, Rich Heritage, and Unforgettable Escapes

LONNIE L. REED

TABLE OF CONTENTS

Santorini

1. Open the Camera app or
Google   Lens of your Phone.

2. Point the camera at the QR
code.

3. Wait for a pop-up notification
to appear.

4. Tap the notification, and the
map link will open directly in
your map app.

Scan to
View Map

Greek Islands

1. Open the Camera app or
Google   Lens of your Phone.

2. Point the camera at the QR
code.

3. Wait for a pop-up notification
to appear.

4. Tap the notification, and the
map link will open directly in
your map app.

INTRODUCTION

Welcome to the beautiful **Greek Islands**, one of the most amazing places to visit in the world. Located in the Aegean and Ionian Seas, these islands offer stunning views, rich history, delicious food, and friendly locals. Whether you want to relax on beaches, explore ancient ruins, or enjoy local culture, the Greek Islands have something for everyone.

In this guide, you'll find the best tips, recommendations, and insider advice to help you make the most of your trip in 2025-2026. Whether you're planning a short getaway or a longer stay, this guide will show you how to explore the Greek Islands like a pro.

WHY VISIT THE GREEK ISLANDS IN 2025-2026?

There are many reasons why the Greek Islands are the perfect place to visit in 2025-2026. Here are a few key reasons:

1. Improved Travel Experience

In recent years, the islands have made lots of improvements to make your visit even better. Transportation, accommodations, and tourism services have all been upgraded to offer visitors a more

3

comfortable experience. Plus, the islands are becoming more eco-friendly, which helps preserve their beauty.

2. Less Crowded, More Authentic

While the Greek Islands are still popular, many people are now visiting less crowded islands or going during the off-season, meaning you can experience the islands without large crowds. This makes for a more peaceful and authentic trip.

3. Mix of Tradition and Modern Luxury

The Greek Islands offer a perfect balance of ancient traditions and modern luxury. You can explore ancient ruins during the day and enjoy modern amenities, fine dining, and beautiful hotels in the evening.

4. Cultural Events and Festivals

Every year, the islands host many exciting cultural events like music festivals, local dances, and traditional celebrations. In 2025-2026, there will be even more events to enjoy, giving you a chance to experience the local culture in a fun way.

5. Adventure and Nature

The Greek Islands are perfect for outdoor lovers. There are endless activities to do, like hiking, diving, and sailing. Whether you're exploring caves, walking through scenic trails, or relaxing on a quiet beach, the Greek Islands offer a lot of natural beauty and adventure.

HOW TO USE THIS GUIDE

This guide is here to help you plan and enjoy your trip to the Greek Islands. Here's how you can make the most of it:

- **Island Highlights**: Each chapter gives you detailed information about the best islands to visit, what to see, and what to do. We cover everything from popular tourist spots to hidden gems that only locals know about.

- **Itineraries for Every Traveler**: Whether you're looking for a quick trip, a family vacation, or an adventurous experience, we've included ready-made itineraries for different types of travelers. You can follow them as they are or adjust them to suit your style.

- **Practical Information**: We provide all the useful information you need, from how to get to the islands to transportation options. You'll also find tips on accommodation, food, and seasonal events.

- **Local Insights**: This guide doesn't just cover the tourist hotspots; it also highlights local traditions, unique places to visit, and hidden treasures that make the Greek Islands so special.

- **Maps and Travel Routes**: To make getting around easier, this guide includes maps and suggested routes for traveling between the islands.

- **Safety Tips**: We also provide essential safety advice and emergency contacts to help you have a smooth and enjoyable trip.

QUICK OVERVIEW OF THE GREEK ISLANDS

The **Greek Islands** are part of Greece and are located in the Aegean and Ionian Seas. There are more than **200 islands**, and they are grouped into different regions:

- **The Cyclades**: Famous for their white buildings and blue domes. Islands like **Santorini**, **Mykonos**, and **Naxos** are here.

- **The Dodecanese**: Known for ancient history. **Rhodes** and **Kos** are the most famous.

- **The Ionian Islands**: These islands are green and lush, like **Corfu** and **Kefalonia**.

- **Crete**: The largest island with beautiful beaches and ancient ruins.

- **The Saronic Islands**: Close to Athens, perfect for a quick trip. **Hydra** and **Spetses** are popular.

- **The Sporades**: These islands are quieter, like **Skiathos** and **Skopelos**.

Each island has its own charm, offering everything from history and adventure to relaxation.

GETTING READY FOR YOUR GREEK ISLAND ADVENTURE

BEST TIME TO VISIT

The **Greek Islands** are great to visit anytime, but the best time depends on what you like to do.

1. High Season (June to August)

- **Weather**: It's very warm, between 80°F (27°C) and 95°F (35°C).

- **Crowds**: This is the busiest time, especially in **Santorini** and **Mykonos**. There will be many tourists, and prices are higher.

- **Pros**: Great for beach days and partying.

- **Cons**: Lots of people and more expensive.

2. Shoulder Season (April to May, September to October)

- **Weather**: Pleasant weather, around 60°F (15°C) to 75°F (24°C).

- **Crowds**: Fewer tourists, so it's a good time to explore.

- **Pros**: Cheaper and quieter.

- **Cons**: Some places might be closed in April, and the water could be cooler for swimming.

3. Low Season (November to March)

- **Weather**: Cooler, with temperatures between 50°F (10°C) and 65°F (18°C). It might rain sometimes.

- **Crowds**: Few tourists. Some places may be closed or quieter.

- **Pros**: Lowest prices.

- **Cons**: Cold weather and fewer things to do.

Best Time to Visit:

The **shoulder season** (April-May or September-October) is best for good weather and fewer tourists.

HOW TO GET THERE

There are several ways to get to the **Greek Islands**.

1. Flights to Greece

- **Main Airports**: The main airports are in **Athens**, **Thessaloniki**, and **Heraklion** (in **Crete**). Most international flights go to **Athens**.

- **Direct Flights**: Many cities in Europe, like **London**, **Rome**, and **Paris**, have direct flights to Athens.

- **Domestic Flights**: After arriving in Athens, you can take a short flight to islands like **Santorini**, **Mykonos**, **Crete**, and **Rhodes**. The flights are quick, usually around 45 minutes to 1.5 hours.

2. Ferries Between Islands

- **Ferries** are a popular way to travel. Most ferries leave from **Piraeus Port** in Athens and go to many islands.

- **Types of Ferries**: High-speed ferries are faster but more expensive, while regular ferries are cheaper and slower. Both are comfortable and offer food and drinks.

- **Island Hopping**: Ferries make it easy to visit multiple islands. You can book tickets online using sites like **Ferryhopper**.

3. Cruise Options

- **Cruises**: Many cruise ships, like **MSC Cruises** and **Royal Caribbean**, offer trips to the Greek Islands.

- **Private Yachts**: You can also rent a private yacht to visit the islands if you want a more personal experience.

TRANSPORTATION AROUND THE ISLANDS

Once you're on the islands, getting around is easy, but it depends on the island.

1. Public Transportation

- **Buses**: Many islands, like **Santorini**, **Crete**, and **Mykonos**, have buses that go between towns and beaches.

- **Taxis**: Taxis are available, but they can be hard to find during busy times. You can use taxi apps like **Beat** to book rides.

2. Renting a Car or Scooter

- **Car Rentals**: Renting a car is great for exploring bigger islands like **Crete** and **Rhodes**, where things are spread out. It's best to book a car in advance, especially during busy months.

- **Scooters and ATVs**: Scooters and ATVs are popular on smaller islands like **Mykonos** for a fun way to get around.

3. Walking and Biking

- Many islands, like **Oia** (Santorini), are best explored on foot since the streets are narrow and charming.

- **Biking** is a great way to see the islands, especially places like **Naxos**.

TRAVEL SAFETY TIPS AND CULTURAL ETIQUETTE

Travel Safety Tips:

- **Health Insurance**: Make sure you have travel insurance that covers you while in Greece. Medical care is good, but it can be expensive without insurance.

- **Emergency Numbers**: The emergency number for police, fire, and medical help is **112** in Greece.

- **Pickpockets**: Be careful with your things in busy tourist spots. Keep valuables in a safe place and be aware of your surroundings.

Cultural Etiquette:

- **Greetings**: Greeks are friendly. You can shake hands when meeting, and close friends might kiss on both cheeks.

- **Dress Code**: Dress casually but respect local customs, especially when visiting churches or religious sites.

- **Tipping**: Tipping is nice, but not required. A 5-10% tip is common in restaurants if service isn't included.

- **Respect Traditions**: Be respectful of local customs, especially during religious holidays or when visiting small villages.

VISA REQUIREMENTS

Most visitors to the **Greek Islands** will need to follow the visa rules for **Greece** as part of the **Schengen Area**.

1. Schengen Visa

- If you're from a non-EU country, you may need a **Schengen visa** to enter Greece. This visa allows you to stay for up to 90 days in 180 days.

- Travelers from countries like **the USA**, **Canada**, and **Australia** do not need a visa for up to 90 days.

2. Visa Exemptions

- If you're from the **EU**, you don't need a visa.

3. Applying for a Visa

- If you need a visa, apply at a Greek embassy or consulate before your trip. You will need documents like hotel bookings, travel insurance, and flight tickets.

CURRENCY, LANGUAGE, AND USEFUL PHRASES

Currency:

- The **Euro (€)** is used in Greece. Credit cards are widely accepted, but it's a good idea to carry some cash for smaller shops.

Language:

- The official language is **Greek**, but English is commonly spoken in tourist areas. Signs, menus, and brochures are usually in both languages.

Useful Phrases:

- **Hello** – Χαίρετε (Cheretete) or Γειά σας (Yia sas)

- **Thank you** – Ευχαριστώ (Efcharisto)

- **Please** – Παρακαλώ (Parakalo)

- **How much is this?** – Πόσοκοστίζει αυτό; (Poso kostizeiafto?)

- **Where is the bathroom?** – Πουείναι η τουαλέτα; (Pou einaiitoualeta?)

- **Goodbye** – Αντίο (Adio)

- **Yes** – Ναί (Ne)

- **No** – Όχι (Ochi)

TOP GREEK ISLANDS TO VISIT

The **Greek Islands** are famous for their beauty and history. Each island has something different to offer. Whether you want amazing views, ancient ruins, beautiful beaches, or fun nightlife, there's an island for you. Here are some of the best islands to visit:

SANTORINI

Why Visit Santorini?

Santorini is famous for its breathtaking views, white buildings with blue domes, and spectacular sunsets. It's perfect for couples, photographers, and anyone who loves beauty and charm.

Top Things to Do:

- **Oia Village**: Famous for its stunning sunsets and lovely streets.

- **Fira Town**: The main town with great views, shopping, and food.

- **Kamari and Perissa Beaches**: Relax on the island's unique black sand beaches.

- **Akrotiri**: Visit the ancient ruins of a Minoan city destroyed by a volcanic eruption.

Location: **Santorini**, Cyclades, Greece

Website: www.santorini.com

MYKONOS

Why Visit Mykonos?

Mykonos is known for its lively party scene, glamorous resorts, and beautiful beaches. It's perfect for anyone looking for a fun and upscale vacation with great nightlife.

Top Things to Do:

- **Mykonos Town (Chora)**: Explore narrow streets, chic boutiques, and windmills.

- **Super Paradise Beach**: A beach famous for its party vibe and beach clubs.

- **Delos Island**: Visit the nearby island full of ancient ruins.

- **Nightlife**: Enjoy nightclubs like **Cavo Paradiso** and **Skandinavian Bar**.

Location: **Mykonos**, Cyclades, Greece

Website: www.mykonos.gr

CRETE

Why Visit Crete?

Crete is the largest Greek island and offers a mix of ancient history, charming villages, and beautiful beaches. It's perfect for those who want to experience both culture and nature.

Top Things to Do:

- **Knossos Palace**: Visit the ancient ruins of the Minoan civilization.

- **Samaria Gorge**: Go hiking through a beautiful national park.

- **Chania Old Town**: Wander through a charming town with narrow streets and waterfront cafes.

- **Elafonissi Beach**: Relax on this beautiful beach with pink sand.

Location: **Crete**, Greece

Website: www.incrediblecrete.gr

RHODES

Why Visit Rhodes?

Rhodes is full of ancient history, medieval architecture, and relaxing beaches. It's great for history lovers and beachgoers alike.

Top Things to Do:

- **Rhodes Old Town**: A UNESCO World Heritage site with medieval streets and impressive fortresses.

- **Lindos Acropolis**: Visit the ancient ruins of this beautiful hilltop site.

- **Prasonisi Beach**: A great spot for windsurfing and beach lovers.

- **Valley of the Butterflies**: A peaceful park with beautiful trails and nature.

Location: **Rhodes**, Dodecanese, Greece

Website: www.rhodes.gr

NAXOS

Why Visit Naxos?

Naxos is a quieter island that offers beautiful beaches, ancient sites, and charming villages. It's perfect for those looking for an authentic Greek experience away from the crowds.

Top Things to Do:

- **Portara**: The impressive ancient gate of the Temple of Apollo.

- **Agios Prokopios Beach**: A long sandy beach with clear water.

- **Naxos Town (Chora)**: Explore the town with its winding streets and historic castle.

- **Temple of Demeter**: Visit the ancient ruins dedicated to the goddess Demeter.

Location: **Naxos**, Cyclades, Greece

Website: www.naxos.gr

MUST-SEE SIGHTS AND EXPERIENCES

The **Greek Islands** offer many amazing things to see and do. Whether you're into history, nature, or stunning views, here are five must-see experiences you shouldn't miss:

ANCIENT RUINS AND HISTORICAL SITES

Greece is full of ancient history, and the islands are home to some incredible ruins and historical sites. You'll feel like you're stepping back in time as you explore these landmarks.

Top Sites:

- **Delos Island**: A small island near Mykonos with ruins of temples and homes from the ancient Greeks.

- **Knossos Palace** (Crete): A huge palace from the Minoan civilization, with beautiful frescoes and old buildings.

- **Lindos Acropolis** (Rhodes): A hilltop site with ancient ruins and breathtaking views of the sea.

Best for: History lovers and anyone interested in ancient Greece.

PRISTINE BEACHES AND CRYSTAL-CLEAR WATERS

The **Greek Islands** are known for their amazing beaches. With clear waters and soft sand, they are perfect for swimming, sunbathing, and relaxing.

Top Beaches:

- **Elafonissi Beach** (Crete): Famous for its pink sand and calm, shallow waters.

- **Navagio Beach** (Zakynthos): A stunning beach with a shipwreck and cliffs surrounding it.

- **Agios Prokopios Beach** (Naxos): A quiet beach with clear, warm water, great for swimming.

Best for: Beach lovers and anyone who enjoys relaxing by the water.

HIKING THE CALDERA TRAIL, SANTORINI

The **Caldera Trail** is a popular hike on **Santorini** that gives you breathtaking views of the island and the sea. It's one of the best ways to see Santorini's beauty.

What to Expect:

- **Hike from Fira to Oia**: The 6-mile hike offers stunning views of the caldera, the sea, and the famous villages on the cliffs.

- **Sunset at Oia**: If you reach Oia at sunset, you'll be treated to one of the most beautiful views in the world.

Best for: Hikers, photographers, and anyone who loves stunning views.

EXPLORING THE PALACE OF KNOSSOS, CRETE

The **Palace of Knossos** is one of Greece's most important archaeological sites. It's a huge ancient palace with fascinating ruins and art.

Highlights:

- **Minoan Civilization**: The palace was built around 2000 BC and was once the home of the Minoan kings.

- **Frescoes and Architecture**: The colorful frescoes and the palace's unique design are some of the most well-preserved in the world.

Best for: History lovers and anyone interested in ancient Greek culture.

SUNSET VIEWS FROM OIA, SANTORINI

Oia, a small village in **Santorini**, is famous for having one of the best sunsets in the world. It's a peaceful place to watch the sun dip below the horizon.

Why It's Special:

- **Breathtaking Sunsets**: Every evening, the sky turns brilliant colors of pink, orange, and purple.

- **Picturesque Views**: The white houses of Oia, with their blue domes, make the sunset even more beautiful.

Best for: Couples, photographers, and anyone who wants to experience one of the world's most famous sunsets.

ITINERARIES FOR EVERY TYPE OF TRAVELER

Whether you want adventure, relaxation, or history, the Greek Islands have something for everyone. Here are some easy-to-follow itineraries based on what you're interested in.

CLASSIC ISLAND HOPPING ITINERARY

Best for: First-time visitors who want to see the most famous islands with a mix of beaches, history, and fun.

Duration: 7-10 days

Itinerary:

- **Santorini (3 Days)**: Start in **Santorini**, known for its stunning white buildings and sunsets. Visit the beaches, hike the **Caldera Trail**, and explore the **Akrotiri ruins**.

- **Mykonos (2 Days)**: Next, go to **Mykonos**, famous for its lively nightlife and sandy beaches. Check out **Mykonos Town**, the windmills, and take a boat trip to **Delos Island** for ancient ruins.

- **Crete (3-4 Days)**: Finish in **Crete**, the largest island. Visit the **Knossos Palace**, hike **Samaria Gorge**, and relax on beaches like **Elafonissi** and **Balos**.

Ideal for: People who want to see the best parts of Greece in a short time.

LUXURY ESCAPE ITINERARY

Best for: Travelers looking for a stylish, relaxing vacation with luxury resorts, fine dining, and stunning views.

Duration: 7 days

Itinerary:

- **Mykonos (3 Days)**: Start in **Mykonos**, known for its luxury hotels and beach clubs. Spend your days relaxing on private beaches and enjoy gourmet meals in upscale restaurants.

- **Santorini (2 Days)**: Head to **Santorini** for beautiful sunsets, wine tasting, and luxury resorts with infinity pools overlooking the sea.

- **Hydra (2 Days)**: Finish your trip in **Hydra**, a quiet island with no cars, perfect for peaceful walks and relaxing in stylish boutique hotels.

Ideal for: People who want a relaxing and luxurious vacation with breathtaking views.

Family Adventure Itinerary

Best for: Families with children or groups who want to explore nature, history, and enjoy fun activities together.

Duration: 10 days

Itinerary:

- **Crete (4 Days)**: Start in **Crete**, where there's something for everyone—beaches, ancient ruins, and family-friendly activities like visiting the **Cretaquarium** or hiking through **Samaria Gorge**.

- **Corfu (3 Days)**: Go to **Corfu** next, with its green landscapes and beautiful beaches. Explore **Corfu Town**, visit the **Achilleion Palace**, and enjoy some quiet time at **Paleokastritsa Beach**.

- **Naxos (3 Days)**: End your trip in **Naxos**, with its relaxed vibe and beautiful beaches like **Agios Prokopios**. Visit the ancient **Temple of Apollo** and explore the charming **Chora** village.

Ideal for: Families looking for a fun and varied experience with history, nature, and relaxation.

OFF-THE-BEATEN-PATH ITINERARY

Best for: Travelers who want to avoid the crowds and explore quieter, less touristy islands with amazing natural beauty.

Duration: 7 days

Itinerary:

- **Milos (3 Days)**: Start in **Milos**, an island with colorful villages and unique beaches. Visit the white **Sarakiniko Beach**, explore the **Catacombs of Milos**, and take a boat trip to see the island's hidden caves.

- **Folegandros (2 Days)**: Next, head to **Folegandros**, a peaceful island with lovely villages and beautiful cliffs. Hike around and relax at the quiet beaches.

- **Ios (2 Days)**: Finish your trip in **Ios**, a lively but less crowded island known for its beaches and relaxed nightlife. Visit **Mylopotas Beach** and see **Homer's Tomb**.

Ideal for: Adventurers and those looking for a quieter, more peaceful Greek experience.

CULTURAL AND HISTORY LOVER'S ITINERARY

Best for: Travelers who are passionate about history and culture, exploring ancient ruins and famous historical sites.

Duration: 8-10 days

Itinerary:

- **Rhodes (3 Days)**: Start in **Rhodes**, a historic island with medieval towns and ancient ruins. Visit the **Palace of the Grand Masters**, walk through **Rhodes Old Town**, and see the **Acropolis of Lindos**.

- **Crete (4 Days)**: Head to **Crete**, where you can explore **Knossos Palace**, the ancient city of the Minoans, and other important historical sites like the **Heraklion Archaeological Museum**.

- **Delos (1-2 Days)**: End in **Delos**, a small island near Mykonos with incredible ruins of ancient temples and the birthplace of the god Apollo. It's a UNESCO site with fascinating archaeological discoveries.

Ideal for: Culture and history lovers who want to learn more about ancient Greece and visit important historical sites.

FOOD, DRINK, AND DINING

Greek food is full of fresh ingredients, delicious flavors, and healthy options. The Greek Islands offer many different dining experiences, from quick street food to fine dining. Here's what you need to know about eating and drinking in the Greek Islands:

TRADITIONAL GREEK DISHES YOU MUST TRY

Greek food is simple and tasty, using fresh ingredients like olive oil, herbs, and seafood. Here are some dishes you can't miss:

- **Moussaka**: A baked dish with layers of eggplant, minced meat (like lamb or beef), and a creamy sauce.

- **Souvlaki**: Grilled meat (often pork, chicken, or lamb) served in pita bread with salad and **tzatziki** (yogurt dip).

- **Greek Salad (Horiatiki)**: A fresh salad made with tomatoes, cucumbers, onions, olives, and feta cheese.

- **Dolmades**: Grape leaves stuffed with rice, pine nuts, and herbs, sometimes with meat.

- **Fasolada**: A bean soup made with tomatoes, olive oil, and herbs.

- **Tzatziki**: A refreshing dip made with yogurt, cucumber, and garlic.

- **Baklava**: A sweet dessert made of filo dough, nuts, and honey syrup.

- **Spanakopita**: A pastry filled with spinach and feta cheese.

Best for: Tasting authentic Greek dishes and enjoying fresh Mediterranean flavors.

BEST RESTAURANTS AND DINING EXPERIENCES BY ISLAND

Each Greek island has its own great food spots. Here are some of the best restaurants to check out:

- **Santorini**: Famous for its beautiful views and amazing food. Try **Metaxy Mas** for delicious Greek food with a twist.

  - **Location**: **Exo Gialos**, Santorini, Greece

  - **Website**: www.metaxymas.com

- **Mykonos**: Known for trendy restaurants. Go to **Kiki's Tavern** for grilled meats and great food.

  - **Location**: **Agios Sostis Beach**, Mykonos, Greece

  - **Website**: www.kikistavern.com

- **Crete**: Try **Peskesi** for Cretan dishes made from local ingredients, or visit a taverna for hearty Greek meals.

- ○ **Location**: **Koundourou Street**, Heraklion, Crete, Greece

- ○ **Website**: www.peskesi.com

- **Corfu**: **The Venetian Well** serves both Greek and Mediterranean dishes in a cozy setting.

  - ○ **Location**: **Corfu Town**, Corfu, Greece

  - ○ **Website**: www.venetianwell.com

- **Rhodes**: **Marco Polo Cafe** offers tasty Greek and Mediterranean dishes in a historic atmosphere.

  - ○ **Location**: **Rhodes Old Town**, Rhodes, Greece

  - ○ **Website**: www.marcopolo.gr

Best for: Finding local flavors and unique dining experiences on each island.

DISCOVERING STREET FOOD

Greek street food is quick, tasty, and perfect for eating on the go. Here are some street food favorites:

- **Gyros**: Grilled meat served in pita bread with salad and **tzatziki**.

- **Souvlaki**: Grilled meat served on a skewer or in pita bread with vegetables and sauce.

- **Koulouri**: A sesame-covered bread ring, often eaten for breakfast.

- **Bougatsa**: A sweet or savory pastry filled with custard, cheese, or minced meat.

- **Loukoumades**: Fried dough balls drizzled with honey and sprinkled with cinnamon.

Best for: Quick, tasty food while exploring the islands.

GREEK WINE AND OLIVE OIL

Greek islands are famous for their **wine** and **olive oil**. You can visit wineries and olive farms for tastings and tours:

- **Wine Tasting**: The **Santorini Wine Route** is famous for its unique volcanic wine made from the **Assyrtiko** grape. Visit wineries like **Santo Wines** and **Artemis Karamolegos Winery** for wine tastings with breathtaking views.

  - **Location**: **Santo Wines Winery**, Pyrgos, Santorini, Greece

  - **Website**: www.santoriniwines.gr

- **Olive Oil Tasting**: **Crete** is known for its high-quality olive oil. You can visit olive groves and try fresh olive oil in towns like **Kalamafka** and **Anogeia**.

  o **Location**: **Anogeia Village**, Crete, Greece

  o **Website**: www.oliveoiltastingcrete.com

- **Other Islands for Wine**: **Naxos** and **Paros** also offer wonderful wine tours, showcasing local varieties like **Mavrotragano** and **Monemvasia**.

Best for: Wine and food lovers who want to learn about Greek wine and olive oil.

COFFEE CULTURE IN GREECE AND BEST CAFES

Coffee is an important part of daily life in Greece, and you'll find plenty of great cafes to enjoy your coffee:

- **Greek Coffee**: Strong coffee served in small cups. It's made by boiling finely ground coffee beans with water and sugar (optional).

- **Freddo Espresso/Freddo Cappuccino**: Iced coffee is very popular in Greece, especially in the summer.

- **Best Cafes**: Try **Katerina's Café** in **Mykonos** for traditional Greek coffee. In **Santorini**, visit **Fira's Katerina's Café** for a beautiful view while sipping coffee.

  - o **Location**: **Katerina's Café**, Mykonos, Greece
  - o **Website**: www.katerinascafe.com
  - o **Location**: **Katerina's Café**, Fira, Santorini, Greece
  - o **Website**: www.katerinascafe.com

Best for: Coffee lovers who want to enjoy Greek café culture.

ADVENTURE AND OUTDOOR ACTIVITIES

The **Greek Islands** are perfect for those who love adventure and outdoor activities. Whether you enjoy hiking, water sports, sailing, or biking, there's something for everyone. Here are the best activities you can enjoy in the Greek Islands.

HIKING AND TREKKING ROUTES

The Greek Islands have amazing hiking trails, where you can see beautiful views, ancient ruins, and natural landscapes.

Top Hiking Trails:

- **Santorini (Caldera Trail)**: The **Caldera Trail** is a famous 6-mile hike from **Fira** to **Oia**. It takes around 3 to 4 hours and offers breathtaking views of the sea and cliffs.

  o **Location**: Santorini, Cyclades, Greece

  o **Website**: www.santorini.com

- **Crete (Samaria Gorge)**: The **Samaria Gorge** is a 10-mile trail through one of Europe's longest gorges. It takes about 5 to 7 hours and offers beautiful views of the cliffs and nature.

  o **Location**: Samaria Gorge, Crete, Greece

  o **Website**: www.samaria-gorge.com

- **Rhodes (Profitis Ilias)**: Hike up **Profitis Ilias**, the highest peak on **Rhodes**, for panoramic views of the island.

  o **Location**: Rhodes, Dodecanese, Greece

- **Naxos (Mount Zas)**: Hike to the top of **Mount Zas**, the highest peak in the Cyclades, for incredible views of the island.

  o **Location**: Naxos, Cyclades, Greece

  o **Website**: www.naxos.gr

Best for: Hikers and nature lovers who want to see stunning views.

SCUBA DIVING AND WATER SPORTS

The Greek Islands are perfect for diving, snorkeling, and other water sports, with clear waters and plenty of marine life.

Top Diving and Water Sports Locations:

- **Zakynthos (Blue Caves and Shipwreck Beach)**: The **Blue Caves** are famous for their glowing blue waters, and **Shipwreck Beach** is known for the sunken ship. Both are perfect for diving and snorkeling.

  o **Location**: Zakynthos, Ionian Islands, Greece

  o **Website**: www.visitzakynthos.gr

- **Crete (Elounda and Agios Nikolaos)**: Dive around **Elounda** and **Agios Nikolaos** to explore sunken cities and shipwrecks.

  o **Location**: Elounda, Crete, Greece

  o **Website**: www.creta-diving.com

- **Mykonos and Delos**: Enjoy jet skiing, windsurfing, or take a boat tour around **Delos**, which has beautiful waters and great conditions for water sports.

  o **Location**: Mykonos, Cyclades, Greece

  o **Website**: www.mykonos.gr

- **Hydra (Kayaking and Paddleboarding)**: Hydra's calm waters make it a great place for kayaking and paddleboarding.

  - o **Location**: Hydra, Saronic Islands, Greece

  - o **Website**: www.visit-hydra.com

Best for: Scuba divers, snorkelers, and anyone who loves water sports.

SAILING THE GREEK ARCHIPELAGO

Sailing is one of the best ways to explore the Greek Islands, where you can enjoy amazing scenery, clear waters, and hidden beaches.

Sailing Tips:

- **Charter a Private Boat**: Rent a private boat or yacht and explore the islands at your own pace. Popular routes include **Santorini**, **Mykonos**, and **Naxos**.

  - o **Location**: Santorini, Mykonos, Naxos, Cyclades, Greece

  - o **Website**: www.sailgreece.com

- **Day Sailing Trips**: Take a boat trip around nearby islands like **Delos**, **Ios**, and **Paros** for swimming, snorkeling, and sightseeing.

  o **Location**: Delos, Ios, Paros, Cyclades, Greece

  o **Website**: www.greece-sailing.com

- **Sailing Regattas**: Join a sailing race in the Aegean Sea for a thrilling experience.

  o **Location**: Aegean Sea, Greece

Best for: Sailors and those who want to explore the islands by sea.

BIKING THROUGH THE ISLANDS

Cycling is a fun way to explore the Greek Islands, especially on islands with peaceful roads and scenic views.

Top Biking Routes:

- **Crete (Chania to Balos Lagoon)**: Cycle from **Chania** to **Balos Lagoon**, passing through beaches and olive groves.

  o **Location**: Chania, Crete, Greece

- Website: www.bike-creta.com

- **Naxos**: Naxos is great for biking, with flat roads and quiet villages. Cycle through farms, beaches, and charming towns.

  - **Location**: Naxos, Cyclades, Greece

  - **Website**: www.naxos.gr

- **Rhodes (Filerimos Mountain)**: Cycle around **Filerimos Mountain** for a more challenging route with great views.

  - **Location**: Rhodes, Dodecanese, Greece

  - **Website**: www.rhodes.gr

Best for: Bikers who want to explore the islands and enjoy nature.

WILDLIFE WATCHING AND BIRD WATCHING

The Greek Islands are home to unique wildlife, including rare birds and marine animals. It's a great destination for nature lovers and birdwatchers.

Top Wildlife and Bird Watching Locations:

- **Zakynthos (Turtle Watching)**: **Zakynthos** is famous for **Caretta caretta sea turtles**. You can take boat tours to see them nesting.

  o **Location**: Zakynthos, Ionian Islands, Greece

  o **Website**: www.zakynthos-turtles.gr

- **Crete (Elafonissi Beach)**: **Elafonissi Beach** is home to flamingos and other migratory birds.

  o **Location**: Elafonissi, Crete, Greece

  o **Website**: www.creta.org

- **Skiathos (Bird Watching)**: Skiathos is great for bird watching, where you can spot seabirds like herons and egrets.

  o **Location**: Skiathos, Sporades, Greece

  o **Website**: www.skiathos.gr

Best for: Nature lovers, wildlife watchers, and birdwatchers.

THE BEST BEACHES FOR WATER ACTIVITIES

The Greek Islands have some of the best beaches for water activities, from surfing and windsurfing to paddleboarding and snorkeling.

Top Beaches for Water Activities:

- **Milos (Sarakiniko Beach)**: Known for its white rock formations, **Sarakiniko** is perfect for snorkeling and swimming.

  - **Location**: Milos, Cyclades, Greece

  - **Website**: www.visitmilos.gr

- **Mykonos (Super Paradise Beach)**: This beach is great for jet skiing, parasailing, and other exciting water sports.

  o **Location**: Mykonos, Cyclades, Greece

  o **Website**: www.mykonos.gr

- **Crete (Elafonissi Beach)**: A calm, shallow beach perfect for paddleboarding and windsurfing.

  o **Location**: Elafonissi, Crete, Greece

  o **Website**: www.visitcrete.gr

- **Naxos (Agios Georgios Beach)**: Ideal for kite surfing and windsurfing with steady winds and clear water.

  o **Location**: Naxos, Cyclades, Greece

  o **Website**: www.naxos.gr

Best for: Water sports enthusiasts who love adventure on the beach.

BUDGETING, ACCOMMODATION, AND LOCAL TIPS

The Greek Islands offer a wide range of places to stay and ways to save money. Whether you're on a tight budget or looking for something more luxurious, you'll find options to suit your needs. Here's everything you need to know about where to stay and how to save money while traveling.

BUDGET ACCOMMODATION OPTIONS

If you're looking to save money, there are plenty of affordable places to stay, such as hostels, guesthouses, and budget-friendly villas.

Hostels:

Hostels are a cheap option and great for meeting other travelers. They often have dorm rooms, kitchens, and common areas to relax.

- **Where to Stay**: **Mykonos**, **Santorini**, and **Crete** have many hostels, especially near popular tourist areas.

    - o **Example**: **Paros Backpackers Hostel** offers dorms and private rooms near beaches and attractions.

    - o **Location**: Paros, Cyclades, Greece

    - o **Website**: www.parosbackpackers.com

Guesthouses:

Guesthouses are smaller, family-run places that offer a more personal, cozy experience. These are often cheaper than hotels and give you a chance to stay in a local environment.

- **Where to Stay**: **Naxos**, **Rhodes**, and **Crete** have many guesthouses that are comfortable and affordable.

    - o **Example**: **Hotel Rena** in Naxos offers basic rooms close to **Agios Georgios Beach**.

    - o **Location**: Naxos, Cyclades, Greece

    - o **Website**: www.hotelrena.com

Budget Villas:

For a more private stay, you can rent a small villa. These usually come with kitchens, which helps save money on food.

- **Where to Stay**: **Santorini**, **Crete**, and **Paros** offer affordable villas.

o **Example**: **Astra Suites** in Santorini offers affordable suites with great views of the caldera.

o **Location**: Santorini, Cyclades, Greece

o **Website**: www.astrasuites.com

Best for: Budget travelers who want simple, comfortable stays.

MID-RANGE AND LUXURY HOTELS

If you want a more comfortable experience without spending too much, there are mid-range and luxury hotels that offer more amenities.

Mid-Range Hotels:

These hotels offer comfortable rooms with more facilities like pools and restaurants at an affordable price.

- **Where to Stay**: **Santorini**, **Mykonos**, and **Crete** have many mid-range options.

  - o **Example**: **Hotel Mykonos Beach** offers nice rooms with a sea view, close to **Mykonos Town**.

  - o **Location**: Mykonos, Cyclades, Greece

  - o **Website**: www.mykonosbeachhotel.com

Luxury   Hotels:

If you're looking for luxury, there are plenty of high-end hotels with beautiful views and amazing service.

- **Where to Stay**: **Santorini**, **Mykonos**, and **Crete** have many luxury hotels.

  - o **Example**: **CanavesOia Suites & Spa** in Santorini offers luxurious suites with private pools and caldera views.

  - o **Location**: Santorini, Cyclades, Greece

    o   **Website**: www.canaves.com

Best for: Travelers who want comfort and luxury without breaking the bank.

BEST VILLAS AND RENTALS FOR LONGER STAYS

For longer stays or if you want more privacy, **villas** and **rentals** are great options. Renting gives you the freedom to cook and enjoy the island at your own pace.

Short-Term   **Rentals**:
Platforms like **Airbnb** and **Vrbo** offer lots of villas, apartments, and homes to rent. Renting is often cheaper for longer stays and gives you more space and flexibility.

- **Where to Stay**: **Santorini**, **Crete**, **Paros**, and **Mykonos** offer great rental options.

    o   **Example**: **Villas in Mykonos** offers spacious villas with private pools and terraces.

    o   **Location**: Mykonos, Cyclades, Greece

    o   **Website**: www.villasinmykonos.com

Best for: Those staying longer who want more space and privacy.

MONEY-SAVING TIPS

Traveling on the Greek Islands doesn't have to be expensive. Here are some tips to help you save money:

Eating Out:

- **Eat at Taverns**: Small, family-run tavernas often offer delicious food at lower prices compared to touristy restaurants.

- **Street Food**: **Gyros**, **souvlaki**, and **koulouri** are great, affordable options for quick meals while exploring.

- **Market Shopping**: If you have a kitchen, buy fresh ingredients at local markets to cook your meals, which will save you money.

Shopping:

- **Local Markets**: Skip the touristy souvenir shops and head to local markets for handmade goods, local honey, olive oil, and pottery.

- **Bargain**: In some markets or smaller shops, bargaining is common. Don't be afraid to ask for a better price.

Public Transport:

- **Buses and Ferries**: Public transportation like buses and ferries are cheap and easy to use. Renting a car can be more expensive, so try to use public transport where you can.

Best for: Travelers who want to enjoy the islands while saving money.

PRACTICAL LOCAL TIPS AND RECOMMENDATIONS

Here are some practical tips to help you during your stay on the Greek Islands:

- **Cash vs. Card**: While most places accept cards, it's a good idea to carry cash, especially for smaller purchases at markets or in rural areas.

- **Water**: Tap water is not always safe to drink. Always check with your accommodation or buy bottled water.

- **Local Etiquette**: Greeks are very friendly, so be polite and greet locals with a smile. In churches and religious sites, dress modestly.

- **Best Time to Visit**: To avoid crowds and high prices, visit in the shoulder seasons (April-May or September-October). The summer months (June to August) are more crowded and expensive.

- **Time Zones**: Greece is in the **Eastern European Time Zone (EET)**, so make sure you adjust for that if traveling from different time zones.

Best for: Travelers who want to make the most of their trip while staying practical and comfortable.

FAMILY-FRIENDLY TRAVEL

The **Greek Islands** are perfect for family vacations with plenty of fun activities, beautiful beaches, and family-friendly places to stay. Here's everything you need to know for a great family trip.

KID-FRIENDLY ACTIVITIES AND ATTRACTIONS ON EACH ISLAND

Each island has exciting things for kids to do:

- **Santorini**:
  - ○ **Santorini Volcano**: Take a boat to the volcano and swim in the hot springs.

- o **Santorini Waterpark**: A fun water park in **Kamari Beach** with slides and pools.

- o **Location**: Kamari, Santorini, Greece

- o **Website**: www.santorini-waterpark.com

- **Mykonos**:

  - o **Donkey Tours**: Ride donkeys through the countryside.

  - o **Fokos Beach**: A quiet beach with shallow water, perfect for kids to play.

  - o **Location**: Mykonos, Cyclades, Greece

- **Crete**:

  - o **Cretaquarium**: A large aquarium with sea life from the Mediterranean.

  - o **Water City**: A big water park with slides and pools.

  - o **Location**: Heraklion, Crete, Greece

  - o **Website**: www.cretaquarium.gr

- **Rhodes**:

  - ○ **Rhodes Aquarium**: A fun place to see sea animals.

  - ○ **Lindos Acropolis**: A historical site with great views and easy to walk up.

  - ○ **Location**: Rhodes Town, Rhodes, Greece

  - ○ **Website**: www.rhodesaquarium.gr

- **Corfu**:

  - ○ **Aqualand**: A huge water park with lots of fun slides.

  - ○ **Corfu Donkey Rescue**: Visit donkeys and learn about animal rescue.

  - ○ **Location**: Corfu, Greece

  - ○ **Website**: www.aqualand-corfu.com

Best for: Families with young kids looking for fun activities.

FAMILY HOTELS AND RESORTS

Stay in hotels that offer family-friendly amenities like kids' clubs, pools, and family rooms.

- **Santorini**:

  - o **Astra Suites**: Spacious suites with private pools.

  - o **Location**: Santorini, Cyclades, Greece

  - o **Website**: www.astrasuites.com

- **Crete**:

  - o **Blue Palace**: A resort with a kids' club and pools.

  - o **Location**: Elounda, Crete, Greece

  - o **Website**: www.bluepalace.gr

- **Mykonos**:

  - o **Mykonos Blu Resort**: A luxury family resort with pools and kids' activities.

  - o **Location**: Mykonos, Cyclades, Greece

  - o **Website**: www.grecotel.com

64

- **Rhodes**:

  - **Lindos Imperial Resort**: A resort with a kids' club and family rooms.

  - **Location**: Rhodes, Dodecanese, Greece

  - **Website**: www.lindosimperial.gr

- **Naxos**:

  - **Nissaki Beach Hotel**: Family rooms and easy access to the beach.

  - **Location**: Naxos, Cyclades, Greece

  - **Website**: www.nissakibeach.com

Best for: Families looking for comfortable stays with activities for kids.

BEST BEACHES AND FUN ACTIVITIES FOR CHILDREN

The Greek Islands have many safe and shallow beaches that are perfect for kids.

- **Agios Prokopios Beach (Naxos)**: Calm waters and perfect for young children.

  - **Location**: Naxos, Cyclades, Greece

- o **Website**: www.naxos.gr

- **Elafonissi Beach (Crete)**: Pink sand and shallow water.

  - o **Location**: Elafonissi, Crete, Greece

  - o **Website**: www.visitcrete.gr

- **Super Paradise Beach (Mykonos)**: Good for kids in quieter areas.

  - o **Location**: Mykonos, Cyclades, Greece

  - o **Website**: www.mykonos.gr

- **Paleokastritsa Beach (Corfu)**: Clear water and great for family swimming.

  - o **Location**: Paleokastritsa, Corfu, Greece

  - o **Website**: www.visitcorfu.gr

Best for: Families looking for safe beaches where kids can swim and play.

FAMILY TRAVEL TIPS AND ADVICE

Traveling with kids can be fun with a bit of preparation. Here are some tips:

- **Pack Light**: Many islands have narrow streets and stairs, so pack only what you need.

- **Accommodation with Kitchens**: If your kids are picky eaters, choose a place with a kitchen to cook meals.

- **Use Public Transport**: Buses and ferries are cheap and easy ways to get around the islands.

- **Bring Snacks and Water**: Keep snacks and water on hand for the kids while exploring.

- **Respect Local Customs**: Greeks are friendly, so greet them with a smile. Dress modestly when visiting churches.

- **Best Time to Visit**: The shoulder seasons (April-May or September-October) are less crowded and cheaper than summer.

Best for: Families who want to travel smoothly and enjoy the islands without stress.

NIGHTLIFE, ENTERTAINMENT, AND SHOPPING

The **Greek Islands** offer lively nightlife, peaceful nights, traditional music, and great shopping. Here's what to expect:

BEST NIGHTLIFE IN MYKONOS AND IOS

For lively nightlife, **Mykonos** and **Ios** are the top islands.

Mykonos:

- Famous for its beach clubs and parties.

- o **Popular Clubs**: **Cavo Paradiso**, **Scorpios**, and **Paradise Beach Club**.

- o **Location**: Mykonos, Cyclades, Greece

- o **Website**: www.cavoparadiso.gr

Ios:

- Known for relaxed bars and clubs, especially in **Chora**.

  - o **Popular Bars**: **Skala Bar** and **Corner Bar**.

  - o **Location**: Ios, Cyclades, Greece

  - o **Website**: www.ios.gr

Best for: Party lovers.

RELAXING NIGHTS IN HYDRA AND NAXOS

For quieter nights, **Hydra** and **Naxos** are perfect.

Hydra:

- No cars, just peaceful evenings by the water.

  - o **Best Spots**: **Hydra Port** and **Karma Bar**.

  - o **Location**: Hydra, Saronic Islands, Greece

o **Website**: www.hydra.gr

Naxos:

- Low-key nightlife with bars and tavernas.

    o **Best Spots**: **Chora** and **Portara**.

    o **Location**: Naxos, Cyclades, Greece

    o **Website**: www.naxos.gr

Best for: Relaxing evenings.

TRADITIONAL GREEK MUSIC AND DANCE

Experience Greek culture through music and dance.

- **Bouzouki Music**: Traditional Greek instruments played in tavernas.

- **Greek Dance**: **Sirtaki** is the popular group dance at many events.

Best for: Cultural experiences.

SHOPPING FOR HANDMADE GOODS, JEWELRY, AND SOUVENIRS

Shop for local products like pottery, jewelry, and olive oil.

- **Popular Souvenirs**: Handmade **pottery**, **jewelry**, and **olive oil**.

- **Where to Shop**:

    o **Mykonos**: High-end boutiques.

    o **Santorini**: Unique jewelry and ceramics.

    o **Crete**: Leather goods and pottery.

    o **Naxos**: Handmade crafts and textiles.

Best for: Unique gifts and souvenirs.

BEST PLACES TO SHOP ON EACH ISLAND

- **Mykonos**: **Mykonos Town** for fashion and jewelry.

    o **Location**: Mykonos, Cyclades, Greece

    o **Website**: www.mykonos.gr

- **Santorini**: **Fira** and **Oia** for boutique shopping.

    o **Location**: Fira and Oia, Santorini, Greece

    o **Website**: www.santorini.com

- **Crete**: **Chania Old Town** for local crafts.

    o **Location**: Chania, Crete, Greece

    o **Website**: www.chania.gr

- **Naxos**: **Chora** for traditional crafts.

    o **Location**: Chora, Naxos, Greece

    o **Website**: www.naxos.gr

Best for: Shopping for local goods and souvenirs.

SUSTAINABLE TRAVEL

The **Greek Islands** are a beautiful place to visit, and many travelers are choosing to explore them in a more eco-friendly way. Sustainable travel means enjoying the islands while protecting the environment and supporting local communities. Here's how you can travel responsibly in the Greek Islands.

ECO-FRIENDLY TRAVEL TIPS FOR THE GREEK ISLANDS

Here are some ways to reduce your environmental impact while traveling in the Greek Islands:

- **Use Public Transportation**: Buses and ferries are great ways to travel around the islands. They are cheaper and better for the environment than renting a car.

  - ○ **Tip**: Travel by ferry to visit different islands instead of flying.

- **Walk or Bike**: Many islands are small and easy to explore on foot or by bike. This helps reduce pollution and allows you to see the islands up close.

- **Bring Reusable Items**: Carry a reusable water bottle and shopping bags to avoid using plastic. Many places offer water refill stations for your bottle.

- **Use Eco-Friendly Products**: Bring eco-friendly sunscreen and personal care products, and avoid single-use plastic products.

Best for: Travelers who want to reduce their environmental impact.

SUPPORTING LOCAL COMMUNITIES AND BUSINESSES

Supporting local businesses helps the islands' economy and reduces the carbon footprint of imported goods.

- **Eat Local**: Choose restaurants that serve food made from locally-grown ingredients. It's fresher, better for the environment, and supports local farmers.

    - **Tip**: Try local dishes like **Cretan cheese** and **Santorini tomatoes**.

- **Buy Local**: Shop for handmade goods, pottery, jewelry, and other products made by local artisans. This helps keep traditional crafts alive and supports the community.

- **Stay in Local Accommodations**: Book local hotels, guesthouses, or villas. They are more likely to follow eco-friendly practices and use local resources.

Best for: Travelers who want to help local communities and economies.

SUSTAINABLE TOURISM AND GREEN HOTELS

Sustainable tourism ensures that visiting doesn't harm the environment or culture. Many islands now have **green hotels** that are eco-friendly.

- **Green Hotels**: Look for hotels that use energy-saving practices, reduce waste, and use water wisely. Some hotels use solar power and have recycling programs.

    - **Example**: **Astra Suites** in Santorini uses eco-friendly practices like energy-saving and waste reduction.

    - **Location**: Santorini, Cyclades, Greece

    - **Website**: www.astrasuites.com

- **Eco-Friendly Villas**: Rent villas that are designed to be energy-efficient and eco-conscious. These often use solar power, have water-saving systems, and follow other green practices.

- **Eco Tours**: Choose tours that respect nature and the environment. You can enjoy walking tours, birdwatching, or boat trips that focus on conservation.

Best for: Travelers who want to stay in eco-friendly hotels and support green tourism.

REDUCING YOUR CARBON FOOTPRINT WHILE TRAVELING

Here's how you can reduce your carbon footprint when visiting the Greek Islands:

- **Travel During Off-Peak Seasons**: Visiting in the spring or fall is better for the environment, as it reduces over-tourism. The islands are also less crowded and cheaper at these times.

- **Fly Direct**: If you need to fly, choose direct flights. This reduces the fuel used for layovers and connecting flights.

- **Offset Your Carbon Footprint**: You can buy carbon offsets to help balance out the emissions from your flight. Many airlines offer this option.

- **Sustainable Cruises**: If you're taking a cruise, choose a cruise line that practices sustainability. Look for ones that use clean energy and reduce waste.

Best for: Eco-conscious travelers who want to reduce their environmental impact.

PRACTICAL INFORMATION AND FINAL TRAVEL TIPS

The **Greek Islands** are a wonderful place to visit, and with a little planning, you can make the most of your trip. Here's everything you need to know for a smooth and memorable vacation.

PLANNING YOUR TRIP

Best Time to Visit:

- **High Season (June-August)**: This is the busiest time. It's hot and sunny, with lots of events, but it's also crowded and expensive.

- **Shoulder Season (April-May, September-October)**: The weather is still nice, but it's less crowded and cheaper.

- **Low Season (November-March)**: It's quieter, but some businesses may close, and the weather can be cooler.

How Long to Stay:

- **Short Trip (3-5 days)**: Visit one or two islands.

- **Longer Trip (7-14 days)**: Visit multiple islands. The **Cyclades** (Santorini, Mykonos) or **Dodecanese** (Rhodes) are great for island-hopping.

Best for: Deciding when to visit based on your schedule and preference.

FINAL TIPS FOR NAVIGATING THE ISLANDS

Getting Around:

- **Ferries**: Ferries are the best way to travel between islands. Book tickets in advance, especially in high season.

  - **Tip**: Book ferry tickets online at places like **Ferries in Greece**.

- ○ **Website**: www.ferriesingreece.com

- **Buses**: Public buses are cheap and available on most islands.

- **Taxis/Transfers**: Taxis are easy to find, but agree on the price first. Private transfers are also available for a more comfortable ride.

- **Renting a Car/Scooter**: Renting a car or scooter is a good way to explore, but some islands have narrow roads, so drive carefully.

- **Walking and Biking**: Many islands are perfect for walking or biking, especially in smaller towns like **Oia (Santorini)** or **Chora (Mykonos).**

Best for: Easy and affordable ways to get around the islands.

EMERGENCY CONTACTS AND USEFUL RESOURCES

Emergency Numbers:

- **General Emergency**: 112

- **Police**: 100

- **Ambulance**: 166

- **Fire Department**: 199

Health and Safety:

- **Travel Insurance**: It's important to have insurance in case of illness or accidents.

- **Pharmacies**: Pharmacies are common, but bring any needed medicine with you, especially in remote areas.

Local Resources:

- **Tourist Information Centers**: Located in major towns and ports to help with maps and tours.

- **Wi-Fi**: Most hotels and cafes offer free Wi-Fi, but rural areas may have limited internet.

Best for: Staying safe and knowing how to access help.

GETTING THE MOST OUT OF YOUR GREEK ISLAND EXPERIENCE

Plan Your Itinerary:

Plan your trip but leave some room for spontaneous activities. Each island has its own charm—Santorini for sunsets, Mykonos for parties, Crete for history, and Naxos for beaches.

Learn Basic Greek Phrases:

Knowing a few phrases can make your trip more enjoyable.

- **Hello**: **Kalimera (Καλημέρα)**

- **Thank you**: **Efharisto (Ευχαριστώ)**

- **Please**: **Parakalo (Παρακαλώ)**

Respect Local Culture:

Greeks are known for their hospitality, so be polite and greet people with a smile. Dress modestly when visiting religious sites.

Try Local Foods:

Enjoy local dishes like **moussaka** (eggplant casserole), **souvlaki** (grilled meat skewers), and **baklava** (sweet pastry).

Best for: Fully enjoying your trip and connecting with the local culture.

CONCLUSION

The **Greek Islands** are a beautiful and unforgettable place to visit. With their amazing landscapes, unique culture, and friendly people, there's something for everyone. By planning your trip well, following eco-friendly tips, respecting local traditions, and supporting local businesses, you'll have a great experience and help keep the islands beautiful. Enjoy your time on the Greek Islands and make great memories!

Made in United States
North Haven, CT
01 June 2025

69398208R00055